YOU
FIRST

ALSO BY LEA MICHELE

Brunette Ambition

YOU FIRST

Journal Your Way to

Your Best Life

LEA MICHELE

CROWN ARCHETYPE
NEW YORK

Published in the United States by Crown Archetype, an imprint of

the Crown Publishing Group, a division of Penguin Random House

LLC, New York. www.crownpublishing.com

Crown Archetype and colophon is a registered trademark of

Penguin Random House LLC.

Library of Congress Cataloging-in-Publication Data

Michele, Lea.

You first : journal your way to your best life / Lea Michele.

—First edition.

pages cm

1. Diaries—Authorship—Psychological aspects. 2. Goal

(Psychology) 3. Self-realization. I. Title.

PN4390.M53 2015

808.06'692—dc23

2015004540

ISBN 978-0-553-44731-6

Printed in the United States of America

Book design by Jennifer K. Beal Davis

Jacket design: Elena Giavaldi

Jacket photography: Justin Coit

10 9 8 7 6 5 4 3 2

First Edition

To my best friend, Jonathan Groff:
I could write a whole book on how
much I love you, Jonathan, and how
grateful I am for your friendship.
Thank you for always making me
laugh so hard I pee my pants, and
for being by my side when I needed
you most.

CONT-ENTS

INTRODUCTION

You first. This seems like such a simple concept, right? A pleasantry, really. It's what you'd say to someone who is trying to get through the same door as you at the grocery store. But when you really think about what it *really* means—when you turn it into a personal mantra, you might find that it's actually hard to put into practice. I'm not talking about being selfish here. I'm talking about actually putting yourself first: listening to everything that's in your heart and mind, quieting any nagging or doubting voices, and then putting in the work of making your dreams come true. "You first" is about respecting and understanding what you *really* want—and then going out to achieve it.

Maybe easier said than done. We often go through our days putting a lot of other people and things first—our families, our significant others, our kids if we have them, our jobs. It's not uncommon to slip into bed at night and realize that you did little—if anything—for yourself all day. Those days can become months, and then years. This book is a chance to hit pause, and find a moment for yourself in the chaos of it all, so that you can really get centered and create some separation from all the noise. It takes focus because it can be pretty hard to figure out what you actually want in the first place, particularly when there are a million thoughts whizzing around your head at any one time, and probably just that many opinions from others. It can be an overwhelming "Choose Your Own Adventure" story—or, worse, it can feel like there's no adventure there at all. Which brings me to a practice that I started many, many years ago that has served me incredibly well. It helps me cut through the clutter—to block out other voices and dig deep within—to really get organized both in my mind and in my life. It's a simple tool, and it's accessible to everyone. It's the practice of writing down goals, and asking and then answering tough questions about what I want out of life. Which brings us to *You First*, a guided journal to help you get the best out of yourself. Not only will we go through a series of exercises about every important part of life to actually determine what matters to you most, but then we'll go through the steps to make sure that you're really tapping into your hopes and dreams— that you're really maximizing your happiness and potential on the path to being the best version of yourself.

So why do I think this is so effective? Because energetically, it's a powerful practice. In the age of digital *everything*, not only does it leave a more permanent impression on my mind (there are amazing studies that show how the act of writing connects with the brain in a way that a keyboard never will), but it's really the first physical manifestation of an intention . . . you are actually creating something that exists! By committing your goals to paper—which can admittedly be a very intimidating, and sometimes even embarrassing, thing to do—you are taking a big step toward making them a reality and not just a passing dream. You are also giving them shape and refining how you actually feel—you are creating a record to which you can then be held accountable.

Whether it was to set a goal professionally, like finding a great manager, or just to eat a little bit better, I've always found that when I've taken the time to sit down and journal, I've been more successful at making these goals happen. Hindsight is everything, of course, and so I really only figured out the power of journaling retrospectively—I found a handful of old notebooks and journals and realized that that's exactly where many of my biggest dreams and successes had started. Written down on the page. Get a TV show, buy a home, become a vegan, get a guest spot on *Grey's Anatomy*, get a record deal, learn another language . . . some of these I haven't completed 100 percent yet, some of them I have absolutely. A few might never happen. And, of course, not everything has happened on the schedule I wanted: I hoped for a record deal a long time ago, though it only just came to pass. But I still worked on getting that deal all the time: I found people to talk to, I wrote a song (and then two), I made a demo.

Looking back, it was so inspiring and encouraging to see that when I put things down on paper, and applied myself to making them a reality, dreams that would have seemed utterly preposterous at the time if I had said them out loud came true. As we discussed at length in *Brunette Ambition*, I was told by any number of producers and entertainment executives that a career on Broadway was the best I would ever do . . . that I would never be considered "pretty" enough for TV. I wanted a bigger career, and so I wrote it down on a piece of paper and did everything in my power to make it happen, and what do you know . . . I got *Glee*. Keep that in mind when you're filling out this book. It doesn't matter whether or not people would laugh in your face about your dreams. It doesn't matter if they're dreams that the people in your life might not wish for you. Put this book somewhere safe, keep it to yourself, do whatever you need to do to feel uninhibited as you express yourself on its pages. It should be a safe place.

It's ironic that this has become my way to manifest reality, because I've always found the blank page pretty intimidating: I was never the sort of girl who could just open a notebook and pour my heart out. My brain works faster than my hands, so I'd really rather just talk out loud. I used to love how Felicity would journal through a little recorder. I really learned about the powers of the practice of writing stuff down from the best, though. Every night, after *Spring Awakening* on Broadway, my best friend Jonathan Groff would sit down—before he even left the theater—and write about his night on the stage. Because we were doing the same thing, night after night, it was his way of keeping a record of the time—of tracking the tiny differences in the way it all made him feel, of writing about what he had learned, so that it didn't become one big life blur. It blew my mind that he had both the energy and the ability to process what had just happened so quickly—that he could express it so immediately in words. But whether written or spoken, Jonathan had this incredibly inspirational record of his accomplishments and goals, and I took that lesson to heart.

I remember when I bought my first notebook at Staples. It was simple, black, super-small. I definitely started with lists, and then I began to record funny moments and funny stories. I knew I didn't need to be an amazing writer to make it worthwhile—it was a safe place. To this day, a blank journal is still a little bit scary to me, which is why I wanted to create a book that's partially guided. If you don't know what to say or do—or what you're feeling, or what you want to learn—this book will help lead the way and guide you to where you need to go. This is about the energy of writing things down, of creating a type of vision board, of asking yourself questions you might not have thought to ask. In these pages, you might find that there are things inside of you that you've never acknowledged, but once they're expressed on the page, you know they're the truest things about you. Or this might be a way for you to hold yourself accountable for achieving everything you want. Keeping a journal and asking yourself hard questions about what you really want to get out of your life is the best way, in my experience, to actually help you achieve your dreams. It is focusing, it is empowering, and sometimes the very act of writing it "out loud" is the only thing the universe needs to help pave the way.

I've broken this book down into four sections: **YOU**, **AMBITION**, **RELATIONSHIPS**, and **HAPPINESS**. I picked these subjects because I believe they are a way to really explore how you feel about your future, and with some resolution and empowerment here, everything else can fall into line to help you be the best you can be. Through simple yet fun and interactive questions, quizzes, and blank pages (each in response to an important question), you can work through these sections in order to give some real weight to your dreams. My hope is that you will put some boundaries around things you know are important to you, and discover things that are lurking in your subconscious that are important to bring out and prioritize, too. So let's get to it: **YOU FIRST.**

YOU

In the most obvious sense, we have to start with ourselves: It's classic advice for a reason, really. Unless you're your best self, it's hard to accomplish everything that you want—it's not impossible, but it makes it really difficult to move forward in your life, your relationships, and your work. It's that whole principle that you should put on your own oxygen mask in a plane before helping others.

In this section, we're going to think about ourselves as a big tree—with a strong trunk that can endure anything life hurls its way, and with an even more substantial root system. Sometimes those roots are visible, and sometimes they're buried under the earth, pulling in vital nutrients and water. It's essential that we nourish that tree—that we honor those roots and treat them well, whether they're obvious to the eye or not. A tree simply can't blossom unless it's healthy and strong. If you're going to achieve everything you want in life—not just today, or tomorrow, but for months and years to come—then you must give those roots love.

This is often easier said than done. It is so easy to put ourselves last—behind work, school, friends, the TV. But this section is about making a conscious effort to change those patterns, and establish some parameters, boundaries, and guidelines for how that needs to happen. When we say, "I'm going to take care of myself," that isn't enough: This book is about creating schedules, reasonable goals, and concrete steps toward success!

But before we get into the nitty-gritty, we're going to think about our roots a little bit more—where we came from, and why we might be the way that we are. It can be wildly life-changing to actually take the time to talk to your grandparents about your family history—you might learn that your life is following the same trajectory as your great-grandmother's, or that your love of art, or law, or poetry is something that is actually a familial trait, that you are fulfilling some sort of cosmic destiny. You might learn that you are blazing a completely new path—maybe you'll be the first in your family to finish college, or get a master's degree. I can't express to you enough how important it is to *use* where you came from—that's what makes you unique. And you might discover parts of you that you've never thought to celebrate before. There can sometimes be differences about us that we're trained to *hate*, but that can actually be the most wonderful parts of who we are. This is particularly true when we're in high school, and want nothing more than to be like everyone else—I fully understand the desire to just blend in. But resist! The world is changing, and people's views are changing, and there's no better time to own all those elements that make you completely your own person and wear them proudly. It's time to accept your uniqueness and run with it.

Once we've spent some time thinking about the true essence of who we are, we're going to focus on becoming our best selves, and feeling like our best selves. I can't achieve much when I'm not taking care of myself—it makes me feel depressed, brain foggy, tired . . . even defeated. It can feel downright impossible to start exercising when you've been sitting on the couch for years, and it can feel downright impossible to shake a bag-of-chips-a-day habit when you've come to crave and expect that salty goodness, but it's time to do a bit better. You won't get everything you want in life—that job, that love, that prized role—if you don't think you deserve the best. So give yourself the best.

So much of this book is about resisting complacency, about doing the work, about accepting responsibility for everything that we can accomplish if we put our minds to it. Because change in life always starts with you. I know actors who can sometimes do their best work when their lives are in shambles. I think it makes them feel edgy and dramatic, and that's their process. But that's not sustainable, nor is it any way to move forward. I don't work like that. I keep my house tidy and organized, and I take care of as many of the nagging details of my day as possible so that I can begin work with fewer distractions. I'm hopeful that this will allow me to create a career with some longevity. Of course I've worked and had experiences where I've been disconnected from my family and friends—but being in a good place with them, and having their support, allows me to do my job so much better.

Whether you want to be an actor or not, my hope is that you step forth from these pages with a good sense of who you are and why that matters, as well as a clear framework for self-love and self-care. My hope is that you will become more connected to your family and your roots. And most important, my hope is that you emerge from this chapter understanding everything that's unique about you, and better able to HARNESS THAT "YOU-NESS" AS WE MOVE FORWARD IN THIS BOOK.

PART I

ROOTS

As you probably know, I believe that family is everything. Writing about my parents was one of my favorite parts of writing *Brunette Ambition*, as I've found that really knowing myself stems out of understanding where I came from. Celebrating my roots and my uniqueness is what got me to where I am today.

The truest way to get to know your roots is to take the time to explore your heritage and past, and learn stories about where you came from that you might not already know—or have thought to ask. Besides the fact that this helps us forge a deeper connection with our history, there are often clues from the past that can enforce how we feel about our calling. Learning about your great-grandparents, and what they did to get to America, might resonate with your tenacious, do-anything attitude; or discovering that you come from a long line of painters might reinforce your desire to go to art school. On the flip side, if you have challenging parents or grandparents, or feel a little oppressed by what they expect of you, it can be interesting to try to understand them from the standpoint of history: Maybe they weren't allowed to do what they really wanted in life and are taking it out on you. With a little bit of perspective, you might approach those relationships with more understanding and empathy, without letting it color how you feel about your own path.

I've been on a major quest to learn everything I can about my family—and it's fascinating. I've been grilling my dad in particular, because his side is Sephardic, meaning Jewish by way of Spain. Sephardic Jews spread throughout the world after the Spanish Inquisition, my family with them. Which means that we don't really know precisely where and how we all came to be where we are—but it's been fun to try to figure it out. In fact, my grandmother used to say that we were the culture of whatever food we happened to be eating for dinner: If it was Greek, we were Greek; Spanish, we were Spanish. It's such a fun mystery to unravel. I was pressing my dad the other day for information, and he told me that his nana told him that my great-great-grandmother (there might even be more greats in there) was a witch doctor, who used to concoct all these crazy, all-natural remedies out of teas and oils. Here I am, thinking, *That's ME*. I've had people at work tell me I legit smell like a tea bag, because I'm always mixing up my own little concoctions at home. It's so wonderful to know where my deep passion for essential oils comes from, and to know that it's connected to something bigger and more purposeful. In the same vein, owning and running Jewish delis runs in my dad's side of the family—and I've always felt a call to open one of my own. How fun would it be to cook for everyone? Maybe it's in the cards.

So while these exercises can be incredibly clarifying, they're also just fun! And they will also last, in physical form. While we live in a digital world and for the most part have done a great job of documenting every moment of our lives, the same cannot be said for previous generations. It's important to preserve the stories of your heritage, before those stories are lost.

MY HOPE IS THAT THIS SECTION IS SOMETHING THAT YOU CAN LOOK BACK ON LATER, AS YOU GROW YOUR OWN LIFE AND A FAMILY. I HOPE IT'S A TOUCHSTONE, BOTH TO YOUR PAST AND ALSO TO YOUR FUTURE AND FULL POTENTIAL.

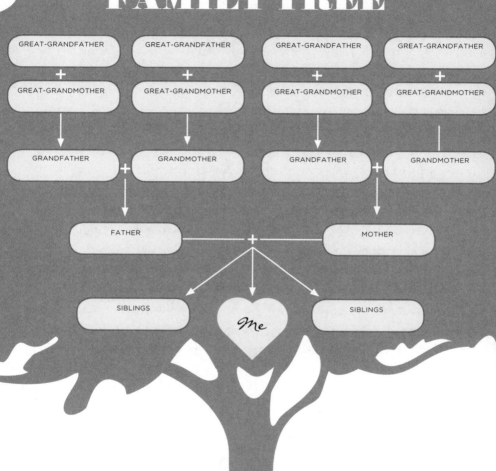

FAMILY TREE

GREAT-GRANDFATHER + GREAT-GRANDMOTHER

GREAT-GRANDFATHER + GREAT-GRANDMOTHER

GREAT-GRANDFATHER + GREAT-GRANDMOTHER

GREAT-GRANDFATHER + GREAT-GRANDMOTHER

GRANDFATHER + GRANDMOTHER

GRANDFATHER + GRANDMOTHER

FATHER + MOTHER

SIBLINGS

Me

SIBLINGS

UNDERSTANDING WHERE YOU CAME FROM

If possible, spend some time with your parents, and ask them to tell the story of their respective heritages.

MATERNAL HERITAGE

Where did your mother's family come from?

_____

_____

_____

_____

_____

_____

_____

_____

_____

_____

_____

_____

_____

_____

_____

_____

_____

_____

How did your mother and your father meet? What were her first impressions?

When and why did your mother's family move to the country you live in now?

PATERNAL HERITAGE

Where did your father's family come from?

When and why did your father's family move to the country you live in now?

_____
_____
_____
_____
_____
_____
_____
_____
_____
_____
_____
_____

How did your mother and your father meet? What were his first impressions?

_____
_____
_____
_____
_____
_____
_____
_____
_____
_____
_____
_____
_____

RECORD YOUR HISTORY

Next, sit down with the eldest member of your family, like your grandmother or grandfather (or both), and record an oral history. Have them tell their whole story, from birth to where they are at now, and have them recount any other points of your family's history that should be recorded for posterity! This can be a powerful experience, so bring tissues.

What was this experience like, and what did you learn?

_____

_____

_____

_____

_____

_____

_____

_____

_____

_____

_____

_____

_____

_____

_____

_____

_____

_____

_____

FAMILY RECIPE

Find the person in your family who is the keeper of the family recipes: Record the most famous and precious recipe here, and keep it to pass on to your children!

Recipe Title

_____

_____

Ingredients

_____

_____

_____

_____

_____

_____

_____

_____

_____

_____

Recipe Steps

FAVORITE FAMILY MEMORIES

What have you learned from your family that has made you, you?

_____

_____

_____

_____

_____

_____

_____

_____

_____

_____

_____

_____

_____

_____

_____

_____

_____

_____

_____

_____

_____

_____

_____

_____

_____

_____

What do you admire most about your family and
what your family has achieved?

What do you admire most about your mother?

What do you admire most about your father?

What, if anything, would you do differently from your parents?

What would you do that's the same?

PART 2

FITNESS

I know, I know: This is probably the last thing you want to tackle at the beginning of the book. Which is exactly why we're going to focus on fitness now: It's easy to push it aside, which means that it's more important than ever to make it a priority.

Fitness is always something in our lives that we come back to, again and again. In fact, if I had to guess, we all spend far more time obsessing and talking about the exercise we should be doing than actually lacing up our sneakers and doing it. Who hasn't joined a gym, only to go... once. I feel like I've done that hundreds of times.

It's pretty easy to get caught up in exercise trend-hopping too, only to find yourself back on the couch: Whether it's waist-cinching tricks that promise to easily knock off ten pounds, or the newest fitness studio offering the newest routine, it's hard to stay focused, find what actually works for *you*, and then stick with it. What I've learned over the years is that it really has to come from finding something that you love. If you love to hike, you will wake up in the morning and go for that hike. You'll take out your yoga mat and go to that class if it's something that you really enjoy.

If you focus on that, you'll soon realize that you don't have to kill yourself on the treadmill; you just have to move. There are no rules here: And what might work for me might not be the right fit for you. You might love the Insanity workout trend that's based on high-energy cardio, while I'll likely pick yoga, which focuses more on core strength, flexibility, and focusing the mind. But hopefully, throughout these pages, we can figure that out, and create some good habits that eventually become something you rely on throughout your life. We'll journal and write, we'll set goals, and then we'll track our progress to be accountable for showing up! They say it takes about two weeks to create new habits, so let's see if that's true.

You very well might surprise yourself. I've always been a big hiker—I could hike for days. But then there came a time when I felt like I needed to get a bit more cardio activity in—that hiking wasn't enough. I didn't know what to add to my fitness routine to really get my heart rate up; I tried a spin class, which was definitely not for me. And then one day, while walking along a trail, I just started to run. And like Forrest Gump, I didn't want to stop. If you know me, or more specifically, if you had known me in high school, the idea of me as a runner would make you die laughing. I was the girl in high school who ran an eighteen-minute mile while the other girls finished their lap in seven. I'd still be struggling around the track when PE was well over. And I've always been the girl who wants to take a taxi to the restaurant that's just across the street. (I was the "Let's just take a cab and I'll pay for it" girl.) So saying now that I'm a runner is crazy. But once I started doing it, I literally couldn't stop. Getting up in the morning and listening to music while I jog has seriously become one of my most favorite things.

I think for me the key to keeping it fun has been that I don't give myself a hard time about it. I don't time myself. Sometimes I run and walk. Sometimes I run five miles without stopping. But because I always enjoy it so much, I find myself looking forward to lacing up my sneakers in the morning.

Throughout the years, I've developed some good habits to ensure that I'm exercising enough. Anytime anyone asks me to a class, I go. That's how I discovered that I like Bikram yoga. Jonathan wanted to try it, and while I was totally scared and intimidated (he told me I was going to pass out and would probably have to spend most of the class sitting), I made myself go with him. Not only did I not faint, but I loved every moment of the class. Who would have known that I was a Bikram yoga natural? Honestly, opening yourself up to new experiences to find out what really works for you is the best way to approach fitness.

SO WHAT'S YOUR RUNNER'S HIGH?

PERFECT WORKOUT FLOWCHART:

Pick the path that you prefer (it can change from day to day).

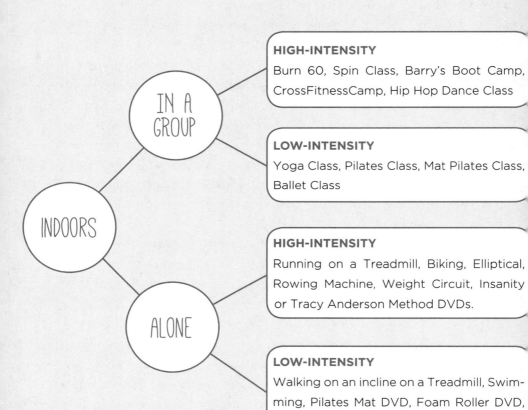

IN A GROUP

HIGH-INTENSITY
Burn 60, Spin Class, Barry's Boot Camp, CrossFitnessCamp, Hip Hop Dance Class

LOW-INTENSITY
Yoga Class, Pilates Class, Mat Pilates Class, Ballet Class

INDOORS

ALONE

HIGH-INTENSITY
Running on a Treadmill, Biking, Elliptical, Rowing Machine, Weight Circuit, Insanity or Tracy Anderson Method DVDs.

LOW-INTENSITY
Walking on an incline on a Treadmill, Swimming, Pilates Mat DVD, Foam Roller DVD, Yoga DVD.

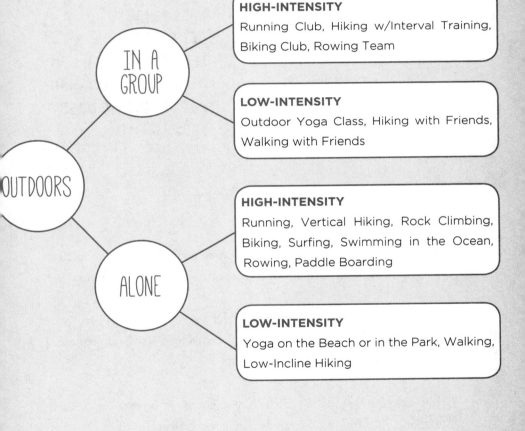

OUTDOORS

IN A GROUP

HIGH-INTENSITY
Running Club, Hiking w/Interval Training, Biking Club, Rowing Team

LOW-INTENSITY
Outdoor Yoga Class, Hiking with Friends, Walking with Friends

ALONE

HIGH-INTENSITY
Running, Vertical Hiking, Rock Climbing, Biking, Surfing, Swimming in the Ocean, Rowing, Paddle Boarding

LOW-INTENSITY
Yoga on the Beach or in the Park, Walking, Low-Incline Hiking

WHAT ARE YOU LOOKING TO GET OUT OF EXERCISE?

GAIN STRENGTH	LOSE WEIGHT
SLEEP BETTER	**GET TONED**
HAVE FUN	LEARN SOMETHING NEW
MANAGE STRESS	TRAIN FOR A MARATHON
BECOME MORE FLEXIBLE	**PUT ON MUSCLE MASS**
LET OFF STEAM	SOCIALIZE

If you picked a majority of **PURPLES**, you need cardio, i.e., exercise that gets your heart rate up for at least twenty to thirty minutes.

If you picked a majority of **EGGPLANTS**, you should focus on strengthening and elongating exercise that's also nice and calming, like yoga and pilates, or weight circuits.

If you picked a majority of **GRAYS**, you should choose social activities like hiking with friends, or dance or spin classes at the gym.

HOW DOES EXERCISE MAKE YOU FEEL?

What do you believe exercise might add to your life?

_____

_____

_____

_____

_____

_____

_____

_____

_____

_____

_____

_____

_____

_____

_____

_____

_____

_____

_____

_____

_____

_____

_____

_____

_____

_____

_____

_____

Do you want it to be spiritual?

Do you want to change your body?

Do you think you need to change your body?

Do other people think you need to change your body? And if so, do you really think their opinion is valid?

_____

_____

_____

_____

_____

_____

_____

_____

_____

_____

_____

_____

_____

_____

_____

_____

_____

_____

_____

_____

_____

_____

_____

_____

_____

_____

_____

_____

_____

_____

_____

_____

Do you believe that your expectations about what your body should look like are healthy and realistic?

What part of your body do you love the most? Why?

What do you think is the right amount of exercise to get per week (in minutes per day)? Do you think that's achievable?

_____
_____
_____
_____
_____
_____
_____
_____
_____
_____
_____
_____
_____
_____
_____
_____
_____
_____
_____
_____
_____
_____
_____
_____
_____

What can you do to make it easier to keep healthy habits? What usually prevents you from exercising?

JOURNAL

Now that we've figured out what routines are worth trying, let's make it a goal to exercise several times a week. If you're new to exercise, maybe start out with two times for the first week, three times for the second week, four times for the third week, and five times for the fourth week. At that point, you are well on your way to establishing a great and healthy habit, and you might actually miss it if you skip a day. As you exercise, jot down your thoughts about it in the following pages (broken out by week).

WEEK 1

What did you do to exercise this week?

_____

_____

_____

_____

_____

_____

_____

_____

_____

_____

_____

_____

_____

_____

_____

How did you feel before you exercised?

How did you feel after you exercised?

Do you feel or look different? Are you holding your self up straighter? Do you feel more connected to your muscles?

Why was it difficult?

Why was it easy?

Do you think it will be harder or easier to do this again next time?

Did anything distract you on your way to do your workout? (e.g., Did you stop to catch something on TV and find yourself on the couch for thirty minutes, or did you go to make a protein snack and end up reading the paper?) If so, can you do anything to avoid that distraction in the future?

WEEK 2

··

What did you do to exercise this week?

_____

_____

_____

_____

_____

_____

_____

_____

_____

_____

_____

_____

_____

_____

_____

_____

_____

_____

_____

_____

_____

_____

_____

_____

How did you feel before you exercised?

How did you feel after you exercised?

Do you feel or look different? Are you holding yourself up straighter? Do you feel more connected to your muscles?

_____
_____
_____
_____
_____
_____
_____
_____
_____
_____
_____
_____
_____
_____
_____
_____
_____
_____
_____
_____
_____
_____
_____
_____
_____
_____
_____
_____
_____

Why was it difficult?

Why was it easy?

Do you think it will be harder or easier to do this
again next time?

Did anything distract you on your way to do your workout? (e.g., Did you stop to catch something on TV and find yourself on the couch for thirty minutes, or did you go to make a protein snack and end up reading the paper?) If so, can you do anything to avoid that distraction in the future?

_____
_____
_____
_____
_____
_____
_____
_____
_____
_____
_____
_____
_____
_____
_____
_____
_____
_____
_____
_____
_____
_____
_____

WEEK 3

....

What did you do to exercise this week?

_____

_____

_____

_____

_____

_____

_____

_____

_____

_____

_____

_____

_____

_____

_____

_____

_____

_____

_____

_____

_____

_____

_____

How did you feel before you exercised?

How did you feel after you exercised?

Do you feel or look different? Are you holding your self up straighter? Do you feel more connected to your muscles?

Why was it difficult?

Why was it easy?

Do you think it will be harder or easier to do this again next time?

_____

_____

_____

_____

_____

_____

_____

_____

_____

_____

_____

_____

_____

_____

_____

_____

_____

_____

_____

_____

_____

_____

_____

_____

_____

Did anything distract you on your way to do your workout? (e.g., Did you stop to catch something on TV and find yourself on the couch for thirty minutes, or did you go to make a protein snack and end up reading the paper?) If so, can you do anything to avoid that distraction in the future?

WEEK 4

What did you do to exercise this week?

_____
_____
_____
_____
_____
_____
_____
_____
_____
_____
_____
_____
_____
_____
_____
_____
_____
_____
_____
_____
_____
_____
_____
_____

How did you feel before you exercised?

How did you feel after you exercised?

Do you feel or look different? Are you holding your self up straighter? Do you feel more connected to your muscles?

Why was it difficult?

Why was it easy?

Do you think it will be harder or easier to do this again next time?

_____

_____

_____

_____

_____

_____

_____

_____

_____

_____

_____

_____

_____

_____

_____

_____

_____

_____

_____

_____

_____

_____

_____

_____

_____

_____

Did anything distract you on your way to do your workout? (e.g., Did you stop to catch something on TV and find yourself on the couch for thirty minutes, or did you go to make a protein snack and end up reading the paper?) If so, can you do anything to avoid that distraction in the future?

WEEK 5

....

What did you do to exercise this week?

How did you feel before you exercised?

How did you feel after you exercised?

Do you feel or look different? Are you holding yourself up straighter? Do you feel more connected to your muscles?

_____
_____
_____
_____
_____
_____
_____
_____
_____
_____
_____
_____
_____
_____
_____
_____
_____
_____
_____
_____
_____
_____
_____
_____
_____
_____
_____
_____

Why was it difficult?

Why was it easy?

Do you think it will be harder or easier to do this again next time?

Did anything distract you on your way to do your workout? (e.g., Did you stop to catch something on TV and find yourself on the couch for thirty minutes, or did you go to make a protein snack and end up reading the paper?) If so, can you do anything to avoid that distraction in the future?

PART 3

DIET & NUTRITION

Diet is another one of those topics in our culture that is discussed incessantly and obsessively. Everyone wants quick fixes and diet tricks, and to know what's in and what's out. And you'll probably watch as your friends waver between extremes. They might be doing a juice fast this week and then snacking on Papa John's the next. We discussed this a lot in *Brunette Ambition*: If you've stayed with me throughout my journey, then you know that I used to think that bagels were the most important food group. It wasn't until I really found healthy food that I loved both making and eating that I began to feel better in all ways. It isn't easy: We're all really busy, and slaves to convenience, and we're often limited in our choices. The purpose of this chapter isn't to preach about the importance of a good diet, or to turn you vegan or vegetarian, or to give you the ultimate diet plan; it's really to train yourself to be accountable for what you're putting in your body. My trainer used to always make me e-mail her what I'd eaten over the course of that day—it sounds extreme, but it was really just about creating a heightened awareness and consciousness. I had someone I needed to be accountable to. I had to write things down and keep track. So this book is here for you now: You're accountable to yourself through its pages.

When I started writing things down, I saw a lot of patterns that I hadn't really been aware of before. For one, I realized that I always used food as a reward. If I'd had a good day, I rewarded myself for doing well. If I'd had a bad day, I rewarded myself for surviving the bad day. A great day at work meant that we should go out and celebrate with grilled cheese sandwiches. A bad day at work meant that I should go home alone and stuff myself with grilled cheese sandwiches on the couch. It was all emotional. But then I started keeping track, and by writing it down I was starting to see that instead of dealing with the emotions of a situation, I was eating my way through them. Just coming to that realization was enough of a wake-up call to force me to pay attention—I wasn't doing it mindlessly anymore, and I was able to change my behavior and my response to both good and bad times. You might realize that you only eat carbs, or that you don't eat when you get stressed, or that you're eating out way too much. It's just worth being a little mindful about it for a while and seeing what comes out in the wash. Once I made the connection that I shouldn't be eating my feelings, I trained myself to take the emotion (there, to some extent, because I'm Italian and food equals love) out of eating.

Let's use this section to see where we can all make better choices and to begin to understand where and why we splurge. In the following pages, give yourself the opportunity to look at what you consume in a day, and think about what you need to improve. One year, I made it a goal to not drink soda for six months—it seemed like a simple goal that I could actually, mindfully reach. (For example, "eating better" would have been harder to track.) But it was weirdly hard: After a long day on set, nothing sounds better than a caffeinated drink for that final boost of energy, and when I fly, it's always been a ritual, for whatever reason, to pop a Dr Pepper; it's very soothing and comforting. But I made the goal, and I wanted to show up for myself—and after a few weeks, I wasn't thinking much about soda anymore, and after a few months, I didn't crave it all. Now, even though it's not on my forbidden list, I rarely drink it. I've replaced it with water—and, as you all know, we pretty much could all stand to drink more of that. In making a conscious and decisive pact with myself, I made my days a little bit healthier. I don't think I could have moved the needle without committing to myself on paper.

In a nutshell, when you write stuff down and journal about food, things that you might not think about—while you're standing over the kitchen sink eating potato chips—become wildly apparent. This isn't about obsessive calorie counting (no calorie counting at all, actually), it's just about attaching thoughtfulness to eating, so that instead of downing an entire bag of chips without even realizing that your hand is moving from bag to mouth, you actually have to think about what you're doing . . . and count the number of times you do it. Hopefully, through this work, we'll figure out how different foods make us feel, so that we can begin to nourish our bodies with the right nutrients. It is very satisfying to be able to look at a week's worth of food journaling and see that you've started to make some really great choices—made all the better because you'll probably feel more energetic and clear-minded as a result of a properly balanced diet.

THIS IS A SAFE AND SUPPORTIVE SPACE, SO BE HONEST!

SETTING GOALS

FOR ONE WEEK, I WANT TO CUT OUT

_____

FOR ONE MONTH, I WANT TO CUT OUT

_____

FOR ONE YEAR, I WANT TO CUT OUT

_____

I NEVER WANT TO EAT THESE FOODS AGAIN

_____

I WANT TO TRY EATING THESE FOODS

_____

I WANT TO LEARN HOW TO MAKE

_____

FOR ONE WEEK, I WANT TO EAT EVERY DAY

_____

I WANT TO SUBSTITUTE FOR

_____

FOOD JOURNAL: WEEK 1

In the space below, each day write a general breakdown of everything you consumed. Did you choose the food because it was convenient? Because you had a craving? Because you felt like you deserved it? Because you were bored and looking for something to do? Also, please note where you were when you ate each item (at home, at work, in the car, at a restaurant, etc.). The goal is to begin to look for patterns.

Sunday

_____
_____
_____
_____
_____
_____
_____
_____

Monday

_____
_____
_____
_____
_____
_____
_____
_____

Tuesday

Wednesday

Thursday

Friday

Saturday

Sunday

7-DAY EATING ANALYSIS

Let's take a look back at our week of eating, and see if we can identify the pluses, the minuses, and how the food we ate made us feel.

What patterns did you notice?

_____
_____
_____
_____
_____
_____
_____
_____
_____
_____
_____
_____
_____
_____
_____
_____

What foods made you feel the best?

_____
_____
_____
_____
_____
_____
_____
_____
_____
_____
_____
_____

What foods made you feel the worst?

_____
_____
_____
_____
_____
_____
_____
_____
_____
_____
_____
_____

Do you think that any of the foods you ate this past week are problematic for you (e.g., made you feel tired, groggy, bloaty)?

_____

_____

_____

_____

_____

_____

_____

_____

_____

Do you find that you eat more out of convenience than out of planning?

_____

_____

_____

_____

_____

_____

_____

_____

_____

_____

Do you eat more when you feel sad?

Do you eat more when you feel happy?

Did you eat more out of the house or in the house?

_____

_____

_____

_____

_____

_____

_____

_____

_____

_____

_____

Did you eat more alone or with friends?

_____

_____

_____

_____

_____

_____

_____

_____

_____

_____

_____

_____

_____

Did you eat more standing up, or on the go, or at an actual table with real silverware?

_____
_____
_____
_____
_____
_____

Is there one food group (meat, dairy, carbs) that dominated your week?

_____
_____
_____
_____
_____
_____
_____
_____

Did you eat a lot of processed foods and/or sugar?

_____
_____
_____
_____
_____
_____
_____
_____

SHOPPING LIST

....

When you make the decision to eat better, it always helps to start with what is in your home. I keep my house mostly vegan and my snacks as healthy as possible. That way, when I'm at home, I know the choices I'm making are good choices. When I go out, I allow myself to indulge a little bit more. So take some time this week to go to the grocery store and look for options that might be a little healthier. Whether that means stocking your fridge with power fruits and veggies, or just swapping certain mainstays for healthier options, it's the first step in committing to taking better care of yourself. Here is my cheat sheet.

....

HEALTHY SNACKS AND GO-TOS: (When I buy things I don't cook immediately, they often go to waste, so I don't go too crazy—that said, it's important to have fresh and healthy options on hand so when I get the initial hunger pangs, I can grab something good.)

1. **Grapes**
2. **Celery**
3. **Cucumbers**
4. **Berries**
5. **Carrots**
6. **Apples**
7. **Avocados**
8. **Pickled Veggies:** Fermented foods are said to boost the immune system and support digestive health—I don't go crazy, as they have a lot of sodium, but they're a great alternative when you want something salty!

9. **Almonds**
10. **Non-GMO Popcorn**
11. **Turkey Slices:** I pick these up from the deli counter and roll them with cheese and mustard as a quick and easy snack.
12. **Sweet Potatoes:** I microwave these with a little Earth Balance butter.
13. **Hummus**

GOOD SWAPS

1. **Vegenaise:** A turkey and cheese sandwich on whole wheat bread is not a bad choice—and when you swap regular mayo for Vegenaise, you're automatically doing something better for yourself, and you won't even know the difference. Vegenaise is egg-free and has far fewer preservatives and trans fats than traditional mayo.
2. **Quinoa Pasta:** Quinoa has more protein in it than normal pasta, making it a bit healthier—it's a great option when you just want to make a simple dinner. If you don't like quinoa pasta, consider brown rice pasta.
3. **Rice Milk:** I actually prefer the taste of this to regular milk. While some people tolerate dairy well, others don't—in fact, some people might not even know they have an intolerance. Rice milk, or almond milk for that matter, is much easier on your digestive system.
4. **Greek Yogurt or Goat's Milk Yogurt:** Sometimes both of these will have more calories per se, but they also have probiotics to aid digestion and fewer fake additives and sugars.
5. **Ezekiel Bread:** Not only is this delicious, but it has protein in it as well.
6. **Almond Butter:** As addictive as Skippy, but much healthier (almond butter has more iron, vitamin E, and magnesium than peanut butter).
7. **Earth Balance Butter:** Organic and vegan—but as great and creamy as the real thing.

And then, of course, **lemons** for **lemon water**. I find that when I flavor my water, I drink more of it! Staying hydrated is the best way to flush out your system.

MY 7-DAY EATING PLAN

Morning: 2 pieces of Ezekiel toast with Vegenaise, avocado, salt, and pepper. (Ezekiel bread is a grain, but also a protein; avocado is a really great super food and a really good fat.) This takes just two seconds and I can eat it in the car on the go: I don't have an excuse for saying that I don't have time!

Snack: Carrots, celery, and hummus.

Lunch: Farro salad with spinach, candied walnuts, and feta. (I usually go for a salad for lunch—most of the time I'm working during the day, and eating something too heavy can make me sleepy. I need an option that's filling but nutritious and energy-giving, rather than something that just fills my stomach and weighs me down. Spinach has tons of protein and is so good for you. Farro is a really great grain. Walnuts also have protein, and because they're candied, they're a small treat. And a little bit of feta is a healthy amount of cheese.)

Dinner: Salmon, brown rice, and asparagus. (This is a super-balanced meal. You can swap that protein for anything you like—chicken, beef. With dinners it's so important to go easy on the bread basket!)

Dessert: Grilled pineapple with agave on top. (I'm not a big dessert person, but when I'm in the mood, this is one of my favorites.)

FOOD JOURNAL: WEEK 2

Sunday

Monday

Tuesday

Wednesday

Thursday

Friday

Saturday

Sunday

7-DAY EATING ANALYSIS

Let's take a look back at our week, and see how this modified week of eating made us feel.

What patterns did you notice?

_____

_____

_____

_____

_____

_____

_____

_____

_____

_____

_____

_____

_____

_____

_____

_____

What foods made you feel the best?

_____
_____
_____
_____
_____
_____
_____
_____
_____
_____
_____

What foods made you feel the worst?

_____
_____
_____
_____
_____
_____
_____
_____
_____
_____
_____
_____

Do you think that any of the foods you ate this past week are problematic for you (e.g., made you feel tired, groggy, bloaty)?

_____

_____

_____

_____

_____

_____

_____

_____

_____

Did you find that you planned your meals better, or were you still making choices out of convenience?

_____

_____

_____

_____

_____

_____

_____

_____

_____

_____

_____

_____

Did you find that you were eating because you felt happy or sad?

_____

_____

_____

_____

_____

_____

_____

_____

_____

_____

Did you eat more out of the house or in the house?

_____

_____

_____

_____

_____

_____

_____

_____

_____

_____

_____

_____

_____

Did you eat more alone or with friends?

_____
_____
_____
_____
_____
_____
_____
_____
_____
_____
_____
_____

Did you eat more standing up, or on the go, or at an actual table with real silverware?

_____
_____
_____
_____
_____
_____
_____
_____
_____
_____
_____

Is there one food group (meat, dairy, carbs) that dominated your week?

_____
_____
_____
_____
_____
_____
_____
_____
_____
_____

Did you eat a lot of processed foods and/or sugar or did you make better choices?

_____
_____
_____
_____
_____
_____
_____
_____
_____
_____
_____
_____

FUN FOOD CHALLENGES

One of the best ways to find out if a food doesn't sit well with your system (all too common these days) is to remove it from your diet for at least two weeks to see if you feel better. By better I mean: you might feel less tired or groggy in the afternoon; you might have fewer digestive issues; you might have more energy; you might see that your skin clears up. Regardless, it can be interesting to try different "clean" diets to see how they impact your system. In the following pages, I'll present three different challenges—try each of them for two weeks, and then journal about how each made you feel.

CHALLENGE 1: GLUTEN-FREE

Kicking wheat out of your diet can be transformative: This tends to be one of those tolerances that's pretty subtle—e.g., people who are affected think it's normal to have a perpetually upset stomach or to feel really foggy in their brains. (Gluten intolerance is very different than celiac disease, which is a serious condition.)

How do you feel after two weeks of no gluten?

_____

_____

_____

_____

_____

CHALLENGE 2: DAIRY-FREE

Dairy is another food that can be very problematic for people—chronic digestive issues, allergies, bad skin, etc., can all be cleared up just by eliminating or reducing dairy. See what happens!

How do you feel after two weeks of no dairy?

CHALLENGE 3: VEGAN

At various points of my life, I've gone vegan—sometimes it's just for a few weeks, sometimes it's for a more protracted amount of time. I find that it's a great way to clean and reset my system.

How do you feel after two weeks of no animal products?

AMBI-
TION

Now that we've done much of the hard work of taking a good look at ourselves, and established great habits through fitness, nutrition, and getting closer to our roots, it's time to start setting one-month, six-month, one-year, and five-year goals.

A

s mentioned, when I first cracked open a journal, I wasn't that comfortable writing for hours on end. So I got my feet wet by writing out monthly and yearly goals for everything I cared about and wanted—both professionally and personally. I very much believe that setting these goals and making these lists allowed me to achieve big things—faster and more precisely. After all, I didn't go to college, which means that I didn't have the luxury of a diploma or the option of trying my hand at different things and developing different life skills (both in class or through internships). That's tough, but it did teach me how to think on the fly, and to be incredibly proactive about my career and my life. Because so many people told me everything that I *wouldn't* be able to do, I used their negativity as a pushing-off block to prove them wrong. I made it a personal challenge for myself to make my dreams into a reality.

Apologies if you already know this story, but when I was eight, I tagged along to a Broadway audition with a friend—not even knowing I could sing, and not even harboring any fantasies of being a star—and landed the role of young Cosette in *Les Misérables*. It was really lucky. But from then on, it was up to me to get myself off that stage and onto a bigger one. I had to pilot my life and my success on my own. While movie stars often do roles on Broadway, you don't see a lot of theater actors making the leap to TV and movies—and so I'm pretty grateful that I managed to do it. Honestly, if it wasn't for force of personality, knocking (nay, banging) down doors, and pushing and pushing some more, it never would have happened. The world was telling me that I really wasn't particularly special—that I was special enough to play vaguely "ethnic" roles in theater—and instead of accepting that as fact, I proved them all wrong. I made myself acknowledge what I wanted—and I made myself put my dreams first. I don't know if I would have ever admitted how much I wanted to prove them all wrong if I hadn't written it down. Seeing it on paper—as a written-down fact—was something to actually act on. It became a real thing and not just something to mull over in my mind.

When I started journaling, I could easily have set tough but manageable goals by saying that I wanted another Broadway show like *Spring Awakening*. It could have been a much smaller circle, and a much smaller career. But part of this process is writing down things that you want that might seem unattainable—even laughable! It's so important to be honest with yourself about what you really want—because if you don't try and make it happen, you'll be disappointed in yourself forever, and haunted by the "what-could-have-been." (Meanwhile, if you don't manage to make it happen, or your dreams change, nobody will ever know—but *you'll* know if you don't try!)

To this end, I wrote down on a piece of paper that I wanted a TV show. And if you want your own TV show, you should write that down. Or maybe you want an A on a certain paper, or to buy a house by the time you're thirty, or to get a VP-level job. Write it down, figure out what you need to get there—all the little steps that need to be accomplished along the way—and then put your life in drive. Be your own person and create your own destiny—life isn't intended to be a passive experience. It's meant to be something that you fully own and experience, with one foot forward!

I know a lot of people in show business who sit around all day and complain that they can't get a job—and I understand it, because Hollywood is a very fickle industry. Being an actor is hard. But I was never the sort of person who just sat around waiting for the casting agents to call. I hustled my butt off. I refused to be complacent. Even when I knew that I probably didn't qualify—wrong look, wrong skill set—I found a way to at least audition. (Every audition and interview is a great learning experience; I suggest doing them as much as possible.) Sometimes, I was shooed away; other times, I was found out . . . like the time when I pretended I could do the splits to make it to the next round. I can't even remotely do the splits; I thought that fear of embarrassment and a huge dose of adrenaline might be enough to make it happen, but alas, I failed—epically.

I would still do it again. And I wouldn't be ashamed to try. It's so easy, as women in particular, to feel ashamed about flexing our talents, about having chutzpah. But in the pages of this journal, I hope you chutzpah it up—I hope you tell these pages about how amazing you are, and about everything you want and deserve to accomplish. You come first. It doesn't matter what people tell you, either. I've learned firsthand that everyone will always be eager to put you in your place, to remind you of your limits, to try to convince you that you're not that special. It's human nature. This book is the perfect opportunity to quiet the noise and get in touch with what you really want, whether it's a huge career, a family, something else entirely, or all of the above. Most important: Please, please remember that you don't have to tell people what you really want—this book is about a relationship between you and your goals, not you and the world.

BESIDES MAKING A LIST OF GOALS TO TAKE ACTION ON, THIS CHAPTER IS ALSO ABOUT FINDING GREAT ROLE MODELS—GREAT ROLE MODELS WHO PROVE THAT WHAT YOU WANT TO ACHIEVE IS POSSIBLE. IN ADDITION, I'VE CREATED SOME CHALLENGES TO HELP YOU GET INSPIRED AND OPEN YOUR HORIZONS AS YOU FANTASIZE ABOUT YOUR FUTURE . . . AND THEN MAKE YOUR FUTURE YOUR REALITY! IF IT WORKED FOR ME, IT CAN MOST DEFINITELY WORK FOR YOU!

GOALS

It's so easy to sit around and fantasize. I want to get married. I want to get a promotion. I want to buy a house. I want to win an award, or be featured in the local paper. This is fun! This is what dreams are made of! But so often, those dreams flit in and out of our minds as nebulous fantasies rather than as road maps to potential success.

In this section, I want you to take those thoughts that repeatedly flit in and out of your mind and put them down on paper—this is your opportunity to really know and identify what's in your heart and your mind. Sometimes it's easiest to do this as a stream-of-consciousness exercise, and then cross anything off that doesn't resonate after. Next, you can start to figure out what's your biggest priority—and also what's realistic and attainable, as you can't do all things at all times. In other words, in the moment, try not to edit yourself as you put pen to paper. This is your opportunity to figure out what you'd love to get out of life, and hopefully from that, some patterns will emerge and you can begin to draw the path to make these a reality.

I wish that this were Lea Michele's "Magic Journal," and that you could merely wish it and have it come true, but real success takes real work! Use these pages to establish where you want to be so that you can start on the path to getting there. I found that one of the most powerful parts of the journaling process was being honest with myself by acknowledging that I really wanted some of the things I wanted. And it allowed me to make the decision to put myself, and my dreams, first. Ultimately, it felt like I was letting myself down if I didn't try to start chipping away to achieve them. Just as in the fitness chapter, I felt accountable to myself to put in the work. Yes, these lists created some structure and organization, but really, it's much more important energetically—you're effectively pointing yourself in the right direction.

As you move through these pages, be ambitious, which can be a hard thing to do, particularly because it's very easily mocked in today's culture—particularly for girls. As you move forward, quiet the voices. And then do that big thinking. I've always found that some of my goals were easy to knock off the list (sometimes opportunities just fall into your lap if you've done the work and are in the right place at the right time); others were impossible not to achieve with a little bit of effort (e.g., to read a certain book or watch a collection of movies); while others were more out of my control. But writing is a way to shape history, and a way to take control. I think you'll find it very therapeutic. Be brave. Be honest. After all, what you write just might come true, so make sure you're pointing your intentions in a direction that feels true to your heart! And, of course, it goes without saying that nothing will happen without effort—and nothing will happen without stepping into the driver's seat and being proactive about your life. If you're not proactive, and you're not paying attention, life can just slip by, particularly because we all get busy.

And speaking of busy, it's very difficult to plan for the life you want to have while living the life you currently have. I had my pre-*Glee* list, but once I got *Glee*, I kept going: I wanted to make an album; I wanted to write a book. Even during days when I was so wiped out from *Glee*, I kept the list of everything I'd like to accomplish in front of me—it motivated me to keep going and to never give up or become complacent. On New Year's Eve at 10 p.m.? I'm writing down my list of what I want the New Year to bring.

It might be that you don't yet even know what your dreams are—or you might be concerned that they could change. Worry not: The intention here is to begin a practice that will hopefully be lifelong, that will touch on all aspects of your life, from family to career. These pages will be markers of what's to come, as well as reminders of all that you've accomplished. There's great energy in laying out a strong plan, and so let's begin the process now!

GOALS

Whether it's about family, work, school, or life in general, use this space to describe what you'd like to achieve in the next month, six months, year, and five years. Be as specific as possible, and list the little things, too. Where do you see yourself? What would you like to happen? What would you like to accomplish? What would you like to see and do?

1-MONTH GOALS

- ☐ _____
- ☐ _____
- ☐ _____
- ☐ _____
- ☐ _____
- ☐ _____
- ☐ _____
- ☐ _____
- ☐ _____
- ☐ _____
- ☐ _____
- ☐ _____
- ☐ _____
- ☐ _____
- ☐ _____
- ☐ _____
- ☐ _____
- ☐ _____

6-MONTH GOALS

❑ _____
❑ _____
❑ _____
❑ _____
❑ _____
❑ _____
❑ _____
❑ _____
❑ _____
❑ _____
❑ _____
❑ _____
❑ _____
❑ _____
❑ _____
❑ _____
❑ _____
❑ _____
❑ _____
❑ _____
❑ _____
❑ _____
❑ _____
❑ _____
❑ _____
❑ _____
❑ _____
❑ _____

1-YEAR GOALS

- ☐ _____
- ☐ _____
- ☐ _____
- ☐ _____
- ☐ _____
- ☐ _____
- ☐ _____
- ☐ _____
- ☐ _____
- ☐ _____
- ☐ _____
- ☐ _____
- ☐ _____
- ☐ _____
- ☐ _____
- ☐ _____
- ☐ _____
- ☐ _____
- ☐ _____
- ☐ _____
- ☐ _____
- ☐ _____
- ☐ _____
- ☐ _____
- ☐ _____
- ☐ _____
- ☐ _____
- ☐ _____

5-YEAR GOALS

- ☐ _____
- ☐ _____
- ☐ _____
- ☐ _____
- ☐ _____
- ☐ _____
- ☐ _____
- ☐ _____
- ☐ _____
- ☐ _____
- ☐ _____
- ☐ _____
- ☐ _____
- ☐ _____
- ☐ _____
- ☐ _____
- ☐ _____
- ☐ _____
- ☐ _____
- ☐ _____
- ☐ _____
- ☐ _____
- ☐ _____
- ☐ _____
- ☐ _____
- ☐ _____
- ☐ _____

ROLE MODELS

I've relied on great role models throughout my life for inspiration and motivation. They've made me feel more confident that I could achieve all of my dreams. Everyone who knows me knows about my love for Barbra Streisand: I talked about her endlessly in *Brunette Ambition*, in part because it's not just a fanatical obsession. It's really mattered to my life and career. Having someone like Barbra as an example always reminded me that I didn't necessarily have to be restricted by my unique looks—that there was someone else out there who succeeded despite not fitting the mold. (Looks aside, I would love her anyway as I'm obsessed with her music: It's on repeat at my house.)

While my primary role model may be a big-time star, role models don't need to be celebrities. Anyone who approaches his or her life in a way that you admire, or who has qualities that you'd like to have, too, is a great option. My mother is one of those people for me. She's been through so many emotionally difficult experiences in her life, including cancer (she just celebrated her tenth anniversary of being cancer free). But throughout it all she's been so positive, strong, and loving. She's also always taken great care of herself, which taught me to have a positive body image, a lot of self-respect, and high self-esteem.

When it comes to work, Ryan Murphy is one of my role models because he continues to think outside the box and continues to drive forward. Even though he was so exhausted from writing scripts for *Glee* and *American Horror Story*, he found time to work on *The Normal Heart*. He has never limited himself or rested on his laurels—he continues to push himself.

You might find a role model in your boss, your teacher, your best friend, or your grandmother (we really learn from those around us who have lived a full life). In this section, we will take the opportunity to ask ourselves what it is about these people that we admire, how we can incorporate those qualities into our own lives, and what we can take from their paths and journeys to enrich and grow our own.

IT'S LIKELY THAT YOU WILL HAVE MANY ROLE MODELS AND CAN PULL BITS FROM EACH ONE TO PAINT A FULL PICTURE, ALONG WITH A PATH TO GET THERE. IT CAN BE SO HELPFUL, PARTICULARLY WHEN EVERYTHING YOU WANT TO ACHIEVE CAN FEEL FAR AWAY!

What inspires you?

Who inspires you?

What is it about them that you admire the most?

How can you incorporate these qualities into your own life?

What have you learned most from those who inspire you?

How is that of value in your life now?

What's a small, simple thing that you admire about them that you can add to your life today?

_____

_____

_____

_____

_____

_____

_____

_____

_____

_____

_____

What's a big thing that you admire about them that you will need to build toward?

_____

_____

_____

_____

_____

_____

_____

_____

_____

_____

_____

Have they overcome tough hurdles or hard times? What did they rely on to see them through? Can you relate?

_____
_____
_____
_____
_____
_____
_____
_____
_____
_____
_____
_____
_____
_____
_____
_____
_____
_____
_____
_____
_____
_____
_____
_____
_____
_____
_____
_____

MIND-EXPANDING CHALLENGES

Sometimes in life it's time to take a break and a deep breath—to *be* rather than *do*—to sit and enjoy some of life's greater pleasures. Even if it's not a particularly difficult time, we get so busy with work and our daily obligations that we forget to look outside of our routines. We forget to add those little treats to our life. What's really pretty amazing is to find things to do that are enjoyable and that we can also learn and grow from. The goal of this section is to empower you to break free from your daily routine—to lift your head up and look around a little bit. Beyond shaking things up, it's important to remain curious, and to be an active participant in your own life! In the following section, you will find some fun "challenges" to add a little color to your day-to-day life. I mean *challenge* in a very lighthearted way—not in a "you must overcome" way. This is the intermission to all the hard work. This is a fun section that will give you the opportunity to experience something that you might not have otherwise attempted.

Back in 2008, I was experiencing a very rough breakup. And at the same time, to make everything that much more difficult, my best friend Jonathan was leaving town. With no boyfriend and no best friend, I was stuck. I didn't have a lot of the personal motivation that I do now, and so I was kind of at a loss for how to cope or navigate those suddenly empty days. So I ordered the largest deli sandwich I could find and a whole pint of ice cream. This is 100 percent the perfect prescription for a breakup, but Jonathan knew I was inclined to overdo it, so when he headed out of town, he left behind a letter.

And in that letter he gave me a set of challenges to meet while he was away. I think he knew that I would ingest sixteen pints of ice cream while he was gone, so this was his way of getting me moving, even if only from the couch to Blockbuster. He told me to watch every Meryl Streep movie while he was gone, and ensured I did it by letting me know that he would quiz me when he came back.

And so I did it. His challenge was simple, but it got me inspired. And motivated. So, in turn, here's a chance to write a Jonathan Groff letter to yourself: What are the things you've always wanted to do but never actually planned? This is an opportunity to give that dream to-do list a bit more structure, rather than just having it floating around in the back of your head as something you should really do someday. For me, one of those things is to see more of LA (crazy but true, even though I've already lived here for six years). Until recently, I had never seen the Griffith Park Observatory, which is embarrassingly close to my house. When I lived in New York, I could count on one hand the number of times I had made it to Brooklyn. I had also never made it a priority to read books, but when I'm in the midst of a season, the last thing I want to do during my days off is to feel like I'm doing hard work, so I've found more creative ways to expand my mind. It might come in the form of a DVD series of all of Barbra Streisand's movies (they're usually playing in my trailer on set) or fun, lightweight books written by other women who are also on TV (Tina Fey, Amy Poehler, Mindy Kaling). Regardless, these experiences make me feel like I'm using my time well—plus they make me laugh, too, and there is something to be said for that!

CREATIVE CHALLENGES

Make a list of ten books that you want to read within the next six months.

1. _____
2. _____
3. _____
4. _____
5. _____
6. _____
7. _____
8. _____
9. _____
10. _____

Make a list of ten movies that you'd like to watch within the next six months.

1. _____
2. _____
3. _____
4. _____
5. _____
6. _____
7. _____
8. _____
9. _____
10. _____

What five concerts would you love to see?

1. _____
2. _____
3. _____
4. _____
5. _____

Complete this statement: Once a week I want to make sure I get out and

_____
_____
_____
_____
_____
_____

What types of food have you never tried that you're curious about? List them below and then find a restaurant that serves each type of food and make a plan to go there in the next three months.

_____
_____
_____
_____
_____
_____
_____
_____

Think about where you live. What are the local things around you that everyone is loving and that you want to try? Be a tourist in your own town. Make a list of the cultural icons and then make a plan to cross them off your list.

Is there something you really want to learn how to make or do? A recipe that you'd love to master? Bake bread? Knit? Make a list of all the new skills you think would really enrich your life and then figure out what you'd like to tackle.

RELA-
TION-
SHIPS

Now that we've looked at ourselves, and our work and career, we can shine the spotlight first on friendships, and then on having someone romantic in our life. It's important to really analyze all relationships to ensure that they're motivating you to be the best version of yourself and are helping you grow. Even though this is an act of looking outward, it's still so important to focus on putting you first: what you really want and need in these parts of your life.

When you take a look at the newsstand—or at society as a whole—it really hits home that we live in a culture that obsesses over the importance of the perfect romantic relationship. It's rare to see lines on the cover of magazines touting stories about nurturing your friendships or celebrating singledom. They're always about finding the perfect guy or girl or igniting romance. And for many of us, being alone might just be the stage of life that we're in. We might be focused on other parts of our lives, and that might be what we want and need.

I also understand why the prevailing dream for so many is to have a solid group of friends and a loving and strong romantic relationship. My friends are no different: They want to go out with the girls and linger over martinis like in *Sex and the City* and have the romance that's on par with Wesley and Princess Buttercup in *The Princess Bride*. Unfortunately, it doesn't always work out that way.

Even if you don't want romance, you've probably found that everyone—your pals at work, your mom, your sister, your grandmother—wants to know if you're looking for that special guy or girl. There's a lot of interest, curiosity, and ultimately: pressure. And a fair amount of stigma attached to being single or not having a plus-one. But keep in mind that there's a lot to be said for going it alone sometimes, particularly if you're focusing on other parts of your life. And remember: It can change in a day. It's always when you're completely comfortable and fine with being by yourself that you find your plus-one.

In this chapter, we'll take a close look at friendships—at how you can be a better friend, and how your friends are, or are not, helping you to grow your life. We'll turn this same lens on the romantic relationships in our lives, and the sort of traits and values that are important. This isn't a book about helping you find the right girl or guy—there are hundreds of books out there that dole out advice on that matter, whether it's acting like a bitch, or following rules, or playing hard to get. This is about exploring what you want and value, and how you expect to feel and be treated within the context of a romance. This is about sketching out your dreams, and how you'd like your friends and your relationship to bolster and augment your life. By putting it down on paper, you can grow a current relationship or find one—and, ultimately, deepen your relationship with yourself.

That relationship with yourself is everything. I've had many periods of time in my life when I didn't have a boyfriend, when I would do the classic *Woe is me, why can't I find someone great?* You never want to think that the reason you can't find someone great is you. But it really was me—I needed to stop and sit myself down and ask myself if I was as complete of a person as I wanted to be. And then I took some time to focus on myself. And I started to take better care of myself. And before I knew it, I found myself in a great relationship. I know that it would never have happened if I hadn't done the work so that the universe could open the doors and usher love in. You have to grow your own life and be a whole you before you can be a *two*.

As you think about all the qualities that are important to you, I hope that you write down something you didn't even know you wanted—that you begin to evaluate your relationships through a prism of deeper understanding. After all, someone once told me to write down my version of a perfect relationship, and I did it. And when I look back on it now, I am encouraged to read that I listed the qualities I've begun to attract in my life: a friend, a buddy, and so much more. Ultimately, we all want to find romances and friendships that make us feel like the best versions of ourselves—that make us feel supported in who we are, fully.

Go ahead and create your perfect girl or guy, create your ideal friendship—nobody is judging you. Writing something down creates the positive energy to bring it to life. We're not talking about the eighties film *Weird Science*, where we're building the perfect "person" from magazine pictures. Be specific, and don't just focus on looks. Do you want someone who enjoys exercising with you? Someone who appreciates food and loves to cook? I wanted someone who would be excited to spend time with both me and my friends. And for friendship, I want friends with whom I can be myself. I want friends who will come over in the middle of the night if I need them, no questions asked. Once you've written down the qualities that matter to you most, study the list closely: If you find that your relationships aren't giving you the support and love that you deserve, you can approach your friends or partner from a place of clarity and perspective, having really thought it through, and explain what you need, and how you're not getting it.

AND LAST BUT NOT LEAST, THIS SECTION WILL ALSO EXPLORE OUR PROFESSIONAL RELATIONSHIPS, WHERE IT'S SO ESSENTIAL TO MAINTAIN GOOD WORKING RAPPORT. AFTER ALL, WE OFTEN SPEND MORE TIME WITH THESE PEOPLE THAN WE EVEN DO WITH OUR OWN FAMILIES.

FRIEND-SHIP

Having a great group of friends—particularly when you live far away from family—is everything. These are the people who make you feel supported and loved, warts and all, who would drop everything to be there for you when you're sad, and drop everything to be with you when you want to have some fun. It seems so simple, really, but I'm sure you've experienced how disappointing it can be when a friend just doesn't come through: Some are well-meaning flakes, whereas others are just inconsistent all around. It's so important, if *you* are the sort of friend who always shows up, that you surround yourself with people who hold themselves to the same expectations. When everything is going well, it's not such a big deal when a friend blows off dinner—but if that happens all the time, and particularly in periods of time when you may be in crisis, then that might be a sign that there are better friends to invest your time in.

Because ultimately, that's what it's about: Relationships are infinitely more complicated than a basic math equation, it's true, but really, what you put in is what you should get out. We all have a limited amount of resources, whether we're talking about time, or money, or emotional energy—so don't sell yourself short by wasting your emotional energy and your time on people who might not deserve it! Find your core group of friends—it doesn't have to be a ton, it could be three or four—and then pour your time into making them feel loved and supported. Hopefully, they'll reciprocate!

When I think about my closest friends, the one thing that rings so true is that they make me feel like the best version of myself, and they bring out my best qualities. If we're honest, there are always parts of ourselves that we don't love so much—these parts might be negative, or catty, or mean-spirited. And we've probably also all had a friend who tends to draw those sides out, so that you feel terrible after you've hung out—kind of like you need to take a shower. You've literally dined out on wine and gossip. This sort of behavior is so infectious (and it can also be fun and funny!) that I try to avoid people who get most of their conversation from making fun of other people. In those moments, it's important to ask how that person betters your life.

It's so essential to have wonderful people around you. Friends like Jonathan enrich my life in so many different ways. My friend Becca will try any crazy workout or fun exercise trend with me. My friend Stephanie is always game to try a new restaurant; that's our thing. Throughout these times together, I'm very aware of the fact that these friends all really enrich my life, that our conversations are exciting and interesting—that our relationships are even, in that we have an equal stake in each other's happiness. The other thing that I love about all of my girlfriends is that they're strong, confident, smart, and successful women, who celebrate and support those qualities in others. They are hardworking, ambitious girls, which means they're great role models, too.

This is not to say that I'm a perfect friend, or that my friends are perfect— we have absolutely disappointed each other. But one thing that I really value is that we're always able to talk about it almost immediately after it happens, and resolve it and put it aside. And these things generally don't happen more than once. The good thing about these moments, and a big reason I would encourage you to always be open and honest with your friends, is that they give you a great opportunity to deepen your friendship: They help to push friendships below the surface so that you're really communicating about the things that matter to you most. And that's important, because if you have the right friends, they can support and help you so that you shine your brightest!

FRIENDSHIPS

....

Sure, we can all log on to a dozen or so social networks and see a survey of our "friends," but I don't know that this digital document is always the best reflection of the people who have had a big impact on your life. This exercise is about writing down all the people who have affected you deeply, whether it was your best friend from sixth grade or a new pal you made at work. You should look here for balance: Are all parts of your life well represented? Or have you abandoned your high school group in favor of a crowd from college? It can be impossible to maintain a ton of relationships from different parts of your life full-on, but it's also good to ensure that you're spreading your energy relatively well in order to create balance. If you spend all your time with your colleagues, and neglect your high school best friend, and then change jobs, you might be a bit bummed that you've let your high school best friend down. In this section, we're going to make a quick list of friendships from the different parts of our lives. Beyond listing your friends by name, add a sentence about why you love each of them and what each has added to your life.

_____

_____

_____

_____

_____

_____

_____

_____

_____

_____

_____

_____

_____

Think about all of your friends, and ask: Who is the first person you call when you're lonely or sad? Why? (For me, it's always Jonathan Groff.)

Think about all of your friends, and ask: Who is the first person you call when you're happy? Why?

What are the qualities about your most reliable friend
that are so supportive?

What do you think are the qualities of a great friendship?

How do your friends help you grow?

How do you help your friends grow?

Were there times when you could have been a better friend? When and how?

_____

_____

_____

_____

_____

_____

_____

_____

_____

_____

_____

_____

_____

_____

_____

_____

_____

_____

_____

_____

_____

_____

_____

_____

_____

_____

_____

_____

What are your five favorite things to do with friends?

1. _____
2. _____
3. _____
4. _____
5. _____

What are five new adventures you'd like to share with friends?

1. _____
2. _____
3. _____
4. _____
5. _____

Ifyoufeellikeyourfriendships are lacking, or you find it difficult to make or keep friends, then there are a few things you can do. If you make friends easily, but they don't stick around, you might need to evaluate whether you're attracting the right kind of people. It could be that you're perpetually disappointing them by failing to "show up" in all senses of the words. It might also be that you're trying to change yourself to fit with what they want in a friend. Regardless, these might not be friendship matches made in heaven.

If you're shy, or new to a town or a job, making friends can be excruciating—and very lonely. It can be so excruciating that you actually shut down, and don't appear friendly or inviting. (Sometimes the reverse is even more awkward.) Regardless, it can be very difficult to acknowledge that you're lonely or need the help of others—I know, because I've absolutely been there! It's much easier to bury your head in a book and pretend like you don't care.

What I've found is that friendships require a fair amount of patience—and that if you remain open to it, like-minded people will find you. This isn't to say that you will make friends if you stay shut inside your apartment. Go and *do* things, whether it's heading to a lecture or a play, enrolling in a class or seminar, or signing up for a sports team. If you love to play hockey, there's a pretty good chance you'll make some friends in a hockey league; if you've always wanted to learn how to knit, see who else shows up for granny crafting hour.

The real way to create friendships, though, is to accept new invitations—housewarmings, birthday parties, and tailgates—even if the invitation comes from someone you barely know! And then you have to force yourself to strike up a conversation. It might sound like hell, but you're in a safe place, with something in common. It's also worth taking advantage of the breadth of social media. If you're new to a town where you know absolutely no one, put it out there on social media, and see if friends have friends who can take you for dinner. I've found that people are quick to open their hearts and homes when they hear someone is new on the scene.

What are five activities you'd like to try where you might make new friends?

1. _____
2. _____
3. _____
4. _____
5. _____

In the spirit of paying it forward, think of five people who might appreciate an invite to go out and do something.

1. _____
2. _____
3. _____
4. _____
5. _____

PART 2

ROMANTIC RELATION- SHIPS

It's probably pretty safe to say that until you're in a long-term, committed relationship, you spend most of your teens, twenties, and thirties wondering what that long-term committed relationship is going to look like—and who your "one" might be. It has to be the biggest suck of time and emotion in our lives, but in many ways, this makes complete and utter sense: Assuming that you want one, finding the right partner is kind of everything, as this is the person who completes the picture, who bolsters and supports you, and who makes you feel like the best version of yourself. It is a big deal, through and through, and most likely, you will love and lose a lot in the process of finding it.

In the past, I've definitely really loved being in relationships, to the point that I would go to the ends of the earth for the person I was with. As I've gotten older, I've started to tell myself more and more: You first. I've forced myself to answer the question of what I really want in a relationship. We girls, in particular, can easily get to the point where we'll do anything for our significant other in a relationship. I've listened to certain music for a relationship, or changed the way I dressed. I really try not to do any of that anymore. I've started to prize being my own person—I'll always put that first in love.

While there are a million-and-a-half magazine articles written about this topic—and just as many books about finding love—I think it's actually pretty simple: You will attract a great partner when you yourself are in a good place. You can date a lot in anticipation of this fateful meeting, or you might not date at all (dating doesn't really make you better at relationships, so I don't know why people believe you have to put yourself out there and date a lot in order to find the one). Instead of spending time studying articles about how to flirt, or how to do your hair, or how to look approachable rather than intimidating, I think that energy is much better spent working on yourself. The time before a big relationship that might result in marriage and a family is sacred time—it is YOU time. And after there are kids in the picture, there's very little time left for just you. Use it well. Guard it. Treat it as the precious thing that it is. Really spend time with yourself and understand what it is that makes you happy, what it is that makes you sad, and what are legit deal breakers for you. Understand what behavior disappoints you; understand the relationship dynamics that you really admire. This is not about looks, or professions, or bank accounts—this is about the qualities of a person. Think about the qualities that you really want. You have to learn how to be honest with yourself, in order to be honest with the person you're soon to love. If you suppress who you really are in order to "be" someone you think someone else will love, then you're setting yourself up for a lifetime of acting—and a lifetime of feeling like the person you've invested yourself in doesn't really know you. From what I've observed, that can be devastating. Life is not a play: You want to be empowered to be yourself, warts and all.

In this section, we're going to really think about the qualities that are important to us—and by putting them to paper, we're vowing to honor them. Try to move past the superficial—being attracted to someone is a given—and think about personality traits and mannerisms that are more telling about who someone really is.

REMEMBER, THIS IS A SACRED SPACE, SO THIS IS A SAFE PLACE FOR YOU TO EXPRESS YOUR DEEPEST DESIRES! IT'S TIME TO PUT THEM OUT THERE!

LOVE VISION BOARD

In these next few pages, write freely about your dream relationship. Be specific about everything (even looks). It's also helpful to think about how you would like someone to make you feel—do you want someone who laughs easily, someone who is very independent, someone who is incredibly nurturing? As you imagine these qualities in your significant other, see how they would make you feel in response (some people crave feeling nurtured, while others feel suffocated; some crave independence, while others would rather be in a relationship where the partners do everything together). If you're currently in a relationship, try to put your significant other out of your mind so that you can answer the questions honestly.

When you think about your past relationships, do any patterns stick out? Were there any lessons you believe you were supposed to learn?

What were the best things about past relationships and the way they made you feel?

What were the worst things about past relationships and the way they made you feel?

Taking everything into account that you've learned from past relationships, what do you think you should be looking for?

What are the five qualities that are most important to you in a partner, and why?

What are the five best qualities that you bring to a relationship, and why?

Are there qualities that you think you should be able to bring a relationship, but that you lack? If so, what are they?

If you're in a relationship, are the qualities that are important to you present in your current relationship? If not, why?

Who can you think of who is in a good relationship, and why?

What are your five favorite relationship moments from relationships past (or present), and why?

1. _____
2. _____
3. _____
4. _____
5. _____

What are five deal breakers for your next relationship?

1. _____
2. _____
3. _____
4. _____
5. _____

What are five qualities in yourself that you must honor in your next relationship?

1. _____
2. _____
3. _____
4. _____
5. _____

PART 3

COLLEAGUES

Wise people say that you should invest in a great mattress because you spend one-third of your life in bed. Likewise, you spend almost a third of your life at work—when you're on set, it's about 90 percent of your time—and so ensuring that your relationships there are strong and supportive should be central to your life and not an afterthought. Sure, there are times when you just want to get to your job, get it done, and head home, but creating friendships along the way can only enrich your life—and sometimes it can be the factor that makes you truly successful.

Not only will these friends make your job a place where you're happy to spend time, but they can also aid your productivity by helping you with time-intensive tasks, or even grabbing lunch for you when you're under the gun. While it's super-important to have strong relationships with colleagues, it's even more important that you're viewed at work as someone who is approachable and enjoys being around other people. You don't have to be best friends with the people you work with, but you have to be a good team player and a positive leader. This will really help you get ahead.

There are days at work when I'm really frustrated and extremely tired. When I go home, I try to check myself and remind myself that no matter what I might be feeling, everyone else is working just as hard—and everyone else is away from family and friends, too. During the workday it's hard to push aside that mean little person on your shoulder that's saying, "I just want to go home." Everyone does. But when I'm able to find that positive energy force within, it really makes a huge difference to the whole set. Working as a team through the hard times, and holding each other up, is everything. And it makes hard work not seem as hard.

When the frustration does mount, it's important to be careful (particularly if you're someone who is inclined to bare your soul) about venting too much about work, as negativity breeds negativity. When you complain about your boss or coworker ad nauseam, it can draw a lot of unnecessary attention and emotion to an issue that's not really a big deal, when you would be better served by just letting it go. It's kind of like "poisoning the well," and it's also a quick way to accidentally become a toxic coworker—so make sure that the venting is healthy!

IT'S OK TO LET OFF A LITTLE STEAM, BUT IF IT BECOMES THE MAIN TOPIC OF CONVERSATION, CHECK YOURSELF A BIT.

WHAT TYPE OF COWORKER ARE YOU?

(circle the answer that most applies)

Have you ever stayed late to help someone finish work for a pressing deadline?

1. Never. It's everyone's responsibility to get his or her work done on time.
2. Never, because I'm usually staying late to finish my own work.
3. I would if someone asked me, but nobody has ever asked.
4. Maybe, but only if it were one of my close friends, and that friend had done the same for me.
5. So long as I don't have plans I can't cancel, I'm always game to help a coworker.
6. All the time—anytime anyone has a need, I stay. I've even stayed alone to finish someone else's project.

When you have to work on a project as a group, what is your strategy?

1. I find out what my share is and then get it done on my own.
2. I'm a control freak and don't really think anyone can do it as well as I can, so I often do most of the project myself.
3. I just do what's asked of me, or what nobody else wants to do.
4. I just do what I need to do to get it done.
5. I figure out what everyone's strengths are and then help divvy up the work according to what makes the most sense.
6. I do a lot! I check in with everyone, too, and make sure that they're all doing OK.

How much do you socialize at work?

1. As little as possible. I don't even go to the office Christmas party.
2. Not much, because I don't really have time.
3. Very little—I keep to myself.
4. I have a core group of friends that I hang out with, but aside from them, not at all.
5. I have friends from across the company—it's good to have allies!
6. All the time! I like to make sure that everyone is doing well, so I do a morning tour to check in with everyone.

What do you do over your lunch break?

1. I usually head out to get lunch by myself somewhere.
2. I eat at my desk so I can keep working.
3. I usually eat in the lunchroom alone.
4. I always eat with my friends—we usually go out somewhere together.
5. I usually eat with different groups, or friends I don't work with—sometimes I'll catch a yoga or spin class, too.
6. I eat with everyone—usually anyone who is around!

When someone at work upsets you (boss, colleague), how do you approach the situation?

1. I just ignore that person, and avoid him or her at all costs.
2. I usually take a sick day because I find it too upsetting to be at work.
3. I just try to keep to myself so as not to upset anyone.
4. I vent to my friends a lot—we all talk about annoying people at work all the time.
5. I try to address the person who upset me so that we can discuss it and put it behind us.
6. I apologize a million times—I hate bad blood!

How likely are you to bring in coffee or treats?

1. Never, that would never occur to me.
2. Never, because I don't have time.
3. Never, because nobody knows my name.
4. I will pick up coffee for a select few if I'm going to get one for myself.
5. I frequently do coffee runs for my whole group, or if an intern goes, I buy the intern a cup.
6. I bring in treats all the time.

If you answered **primarily 1**, then you should probably spend some time thinking about whether your job is the job for you, since it apparently makes you seethe with resentment. It's important to remember that life has a way of putting lessons in front of you, and sometimes those lessons are jobs that we dislike or people we don't love—they're there to teach us something (like how to get along). It's not healthy to treat your work environment and your colleagues with hostility—if you find a way to shift your attitude and open your mind, you might actually find that you like it more than you would think.

If you answered **primarily 2**, then it sounds like your job really stresses you out—it's critical that you begin to look after yourself and establish some boundaries. Ask for help if needed, and confine your workday to appropriate "office" hours. Late nights do not necessarily result in more productivity, so try to work smarter rather than longer. Make sure you're taking time for yourself—e.g., eating well, going to the gym, and creating lasting friendships. You don't have to be stressed and miserable to be good at your job!

If you answered **primarily 3**, then it sounds like you might have social anxiety that could prove crippling. You shouldn't go through life alone! It might be time to find a therapist to speak to who can teach you some tools for quelling any interior anxiety so that you feel comfortable approaching colleagues. Consider signing up for any volunteer activities that your job might offer (e.g., Habitat for Humanity), since that can be a great way to meet coworkers. Speak up in group situations, too, because you certainly have something worthy to add to the conversation, and you will demonstrate to your colleagues that you have something to say!

If you answered **primarily 4**, it sounds like you might be a little clique-y at work. There is nothing wrong with forging strong friendships, but be sure that you're not being exclusive, and that you're being open and welcoming to others. Also, be sure that you're not creating a toxic or catty environment by discussing the people you work with—negativity can be contagious. If you think you might be becoming too involved with a small group at work, expand your horizons a bit—either invite some people you don't normally eat with to join you for lunch, or try doing your own thing a few days a week. Keep in mind, too, that if you get too involved with your coworkers, it can be hard to keep an open mind about potentially leaving for a better opportunity—it can also be crushing if your coworkers move on and leave you behind. There's nothing wrong with making great friends, just make sure it's not limiting your world too much.

If you answered **primarily 5**, it sounds like you're a pretty great and balanced coworker who is generous of spirit and always looking out for the common good. It also sounds like you haven't overly personalized work—that you take time during the day to do things for yourself as well as for people who might not be in your core friend group. This is a great way to keep things nice and balanced and friendly. You also get points for addressing the coworker or boss who is upsetting you directly rather than venting to coworkers, which can quickly turn the workplace into a pretty toxic and negative place. It's much better to nip things in the bud and address them immediately before they fester and become bigger deals than they need to be!

If you answered **primarily 6**, it sounds like you're a fun and considerate co-worker. That said, I want to caution you to have boundaries, both for yourself and for your colleagues (they might not always appreciate the interruptions to their workday). Be sure that you're not becoming the office busybody/gossip, and that your attentions are really wanted. Also, be sure that you're not giving too much of yourself at work—don't forget to take care of yourself in the process!

List some specific changes that you'd like to make now that you're aware of your behavior at work.

1. _____
2. _____
3. _____
4. _____
5. _____

What's one small thing that you can do every day to make your relationships at work easier?

_____
_____
_____
_____
_____
_____
_____
_____
_____

Now that you're aware of some things that you might need to change, try to put those changes into practice for a week or two. Then, journal again about how your work relationships are developing and any progress you might be making.

_____

_____

_____

_____

_____

_____

_____

_____

_____

_____

_____

_____

_____

_____

_____

_____

_____

_____

_____

_____

_____

_____

_____

_____

_____

_____

Identify some people at work who would be good mentors—these should be people you admire, who work really well on a team, and are respected within the organization. Ask them if they might have twenty minutes to chat so you can learn a bit more about how they got to be where they are. The hope here is that they might become ongoing mentors and career coaches, if you strike up a rapport. Record everything that you learn.

HAPP-
INESS

As I mentioned in Brunette Ambition, my father always said to me: Just be happy. It seems so simple, but it's the hardest thing to do, and the hardest thing to really find. Happiness can be quite elusive. Often, we believe that if we finally get the perfect job, or the perfect relationship, or the perfect set of friends, the package will come with happiness, but that's never actually the case. True happiness really only shows its face when you can prove that you're happy alone, at home, with no plans, no relationship, no real distractions.

It takes a lot of hard work to get there, and it can feel a bit scary, but I promise that it

opens up new doors for you to live a full life, and for you to meet people who might herald better jobs and better relationships. Some of the work we've done in this book will help get us there. It takes effort—it definitely doesn't come with the snap of your fingers.

A couple of years ago, I found myself at a place in my life where I was forced to start over—at the very bottom—and forced to rethink *everything*. I literally had to scrape myself off the floor. I learned a lot about happiness in that process. The biggest lesson I learned is that happiness is in you. It's in all of us, just ready to be discovered, ignited, and explored. It's all good, it really is.

When I hit rock bottom, I discovered that I had always confused what real happiness was about. I would be really happy at a dinner with friends, and then come home and be sad. Or I would cook a delicious bowl of macaroni and cheese and then, after eating the whole thing, wouldn't feel so good anymore. I could find things to make me happy in the moment, but I was making the mistake of using things, people, and meals to fill a void and validate me. A lot of us do this without realizing that that's what we're doing. On the worst days, I don't think there was any other way: I really leaned on a lot of people. I said *yes* to every invitation just to stay engaged and distracted until the pain wasn't quite as sharp. But I always knew in the back of my mind that real, sustainable happiness would be up to me. When I felt strong enough to be alone again, I took the time to figure out what would make me feel truly enriched. I found some new, hopefully lifelong hobbies. I found things that I was passionate about, that brought continued and ongoing joy rather than temporary relief. I started to create new patterns of behavior, a new schedule, and new things that weren't anchored with heavy memories. Eventually,

I found happiness on my own. The minute it happened, it opened me up to a new relationship, new opportunities, and a new form of happiness that I am so grateful for at this point in my life.

In the process of creating new rituals and hobbies, I discovered many activities that I came to love (and dislike). Now that the storm has passed and the sun can shine again, these things continue to add sparkle to my life. Unlike the "Mind-Expanding Challenges" sections (see page 146), this isn't about finding quick diversions—this is about looking for those hobbies that can become tentpoles in your life. For me, they opened up doors to having fun experiences with friends and meeting new people. That's why in this chapter I really encourage you to explore finding new passions—all while thinking of ways that you can give back, as that always brings such joy to our hearts.

This is my favorite section in the book, actually, because I think that while it's so important to focus energy inward, it's essential to find the small exterior things that bring you out of yourself. Because it works. Finding true happiness is something that takes a lot of energy, and a lot of time. But once you've arrived, you won't give it up for anything. While this book can't get you 100 percent of the way there, right away, I know from my own past that adding little new experiences to your life will open you up to finding the path.

AND IT WILL REALLY HELP YOU DEVELOP YOURSELF FULLY, SIMPLY BY PUSHING YOU OUTSIDE OF YOUR COMFORT ZONE.

PART I

HOBBIES

You don't have to be where I was in my life—at the very bottom—to take a look at yourself and realize that maybe you spend too much time working and not enough time on yourself. It's easy to put yourself last—we all get busy—but this section is important. Because that hobby, passion, and "you" time is the time that might amount to the best memories in your life. This is real "You First" time.

These don't have to be dramatic activities either, or require a huge commitment of time or money. These are really about passion and opening yourself up to new experiences that you might actually come to love (there might be some doozies in the mix, too). We've discussed a few of these: I was never a big reader, for example, but in the past year I've started reading more than I ever had, and it makes me feel great. I started doing Kundalini yoga because I love Bikram yoga, and I came to love it too. (It includes meditation and mantras, which I absolutely love.) I didn't think it was something I could do, but I tried it and it's now a favorite practice. Of course there were the things I tried that I despised, but for the most part, I discovered so many great activities to break me out of my routine.

I've also started having cooking parties at my house, which is kind of funny, because historically I never loved having huge groups over (just a friend or two, as anything more than that felt intimidating). But cooking for me has become a version of therapy. Keep that in mind: Things that might sound terrible, invasive, or scary to you might actually be exactly what the doctor ordered. One of the best outcomes of this extra time investment is that it's made me better at my job—I don't find myself feeling resentful about the hours spent on set because my life feels like it has so much more balance now.

As you work your way through this chapter, I don't want you to work as hard as you have in the other parts of this book. As you relax into these pages, see what comes forth as something you think you might really enjoy—and then make it a goal to incorporate the activity into your weekly routine.

What does happiness mean to you?

When are you the most happy?

What is your happiest memory?

When did you laugh the hardest?

Keeping these things in mind, what are some activities and hobbies you'd like to add to your routine?

What are five things you've always wanted to open yourself up to trying?

1. _____

_____

_____

_____

2. _____

_____

_____

_____

3. _____

_____

_____

_____

4. _____

_____

_____

_____

5. _____

_____

_____

_____

_____

What was the most spontaneous thing you ever tried and ended up enjoying?

What's the most exciting thing you've ever done? How did it make you feel?

What's something that you would like to share with a friend?

What's the scariest thing that you've ever tried? What was scary about it?

PART 2

CHARITY & GIVING BACK

It's so easy to tune out social issues: It can be stressful and anxiety-inducing to think about big problems—like war, global warming, and poverty—because it can feel impossible to make a difference. And therefore, it's a lot more convenient to just hope that they will never affect us directly, and focus our attention on things that we can control. But one person can make a huge difference. YOU can make a huge difference.

I had never been involved with charities, but one day, when I was living in New York and in between Broadway shows, I was watching Janice Dickinson's reality TV show, which was about models living in the city. In one episode, she told all the models that if they were going to work with her, they could never wear fur. And she had a rep from PETA come on the show. I had only ever heard horror stories about PETA and the extreme measures that they went to, but I was very inspired by the show. And so I went on PETA's website and wrote in a comment box, as just a regular girl from New York. I was not a star, I was just a normal citizen at the time. I was concerned about the status of the carriage horses. I would see them in Central Park, and it didn't seem like a particularly great life for a horse, and so I wanted to know whether they were treated well. I immediately got a response: They told me that the carriage horses were in fact treated terribly. And so I mobilized to help, which was really just the block-and-tackle work of getting the word out about the plight of the carriage horses. It was nothing fancier than that. I've had a relationship with PETA for a really long time. As I got to know the team, I completely changed my mind about them as an organization. Honestly, it made me feel wonderful to do something, and it brought an extreme sense of power and responsibility to my life. You don't have to be a celebrity to do it. You don't have to have a lot of power or money to participate—every person makes a difference.

My mother had uterine cancer, which was one of the worst periods of my life. If you've ever had a close family member become ill, you know the feelings of helplessness and despair that accompany the news. Here was my mother, someone who has always taken care of me, sick. And there was nothing I could do. It was incredibly terrifying and also sad to see someone so full of life, who always took such great care of herself, so ill. When I started working with L'Oréal, I was thrilled to discover that they do a tremendous amount of great work for uterine cancer. It was so empowering to bring even more of a spotlight—through social media and events—to the work that their foundation is doing for women like my mother. It was the first time I felt like I could do something to help in a situation where I had always felt helpless.

As you work through the following pages, take the time to think about issues you're passionate about. And most important, quiet the voice in your head that is saying that you don't matter.

EVERY PERSON BRINGS STRENGTH AND ENERGY, AND CAN MAKE A HUGE IMPACT.

What would you fix, if you could fix anything in the world?

Why is this change important, and what does it mean to you?

_____

_____

_____

_____

_____

_____

_____

_____

_____

_____

_____

_____

_____

_____

_____

_____

_____

_____

_____

_____

_____

_____

_____

_____

_____

_____

_____

How would it bring you happiness and fulfillment?

What charity/issue are you most passionate about?

What's the one thing you'd most like to put your energy toward?

What do you want your legacy in life to be?

What are a few steps you can take to get involved in something that you're passionate about? (Make it a weekly goal to explore one organization.)

If you've been donating your time or money, does it make you happy? How does it make you feel?

How much time, money, or both would you like to donate this year?

_____

_____

_____

_____

_____

_____

_____

_____

_____

_____

How much money do you think you could save per week, per month, or per year to donate to a charity that's doing work you care about?

_____

_____

_____

_____

_____

_____

_____

_____

How much time do you think you could realistically give to a charity that's doing work you care about?

_____
_____
_____
_____
_____
_____
_____
_____
_____
_____
_____

What can you do to make this happen?

_____
_____
_____
_____
_____
_____
_____
_____
_____
_____
_____
_____

PART 3

GRATITUDE

I'm so grateful that this is my life. Every day, I try to remember to stop, and look around, and count my blessings—it can be difficult to take stock of everything that you already have when you're thinking about all that you want to change. It can be difficult to take stock of all that you've accomplished when you're focused on what's ahead. This is the moment to take a breath and reflect on where you are in life right *now,* and how incredible that is. It's time to give yourself a pat on the back. And then it's time to express your gratitude for everyone who is there for you in your life—everyone who makes your days a bit sunnier and bright, who supports you as you forge ahead.

I'm so incredibly thankful for my family, for always reminding me of who I am, and where I came from. I'm so incredibly thankful for all of you, for I wouldn't have accomplished a tiny fraction of what I have without my fans and all of your incredible support. I feel extreme gratitude every day.

I'm in a transitional phase of my life: *Glee* is over, and while I'm mourning the final days, I'm also looking forward to all that is possible in the next few years. And with that comes planning: I'm digging deep to figure out what I want to accomplish next, what feels like the right thing. And you know that I'm writing down all my hopes and dreams for the future.

No matter how long you took to finish this book—whether you wrote right through it or picked it up and put it down a hundred times—I hope you have something pretty incredible to look back on. I hope that it points a way forward for you to take action on your dreams; I hope that it solidifies what you believe to be true about yourself; I hope that it's a road map and vision board for a pretty incredible future.

I'm so thankful that you took this journey with me. As you close this final page, take a minute to reflect on all that you're grateful for, all that you love about your life, your family, your friends, and your job.

And most important, take a minute to think about all that you love about you.

ACKNOWL-EDGMENTS

Mom and Dad: You deserve the biggest thanks for supporting me and always making me feel and know that I can achieve all of my dreams.

Alissa Vradenburg at Untitled: You truly helped me make all of this happen. I'm so grateful to have you as an amazing friend and a champion of a manager. And a big thank-you to Jason Weinberg, too.

Nicole Perez at PMK: You truly are the greatest publicist in the game. Thank you for your support, loyalty, and friendship, and for always accepting me (and picking up my calls even late at night).

Robert Offer and Shelby Weiser: Thank you for always having my back.

Justin Coit, Melanie Inglessis, Davy Newkirk, and Jenna Hipp for being such an incredible team and helping me shoot this gorgeous cover—and for making me feel as beautiful on the inside as on the outside.

To all the amazing people at Crown who were so wonderful in giving me the freedom to truly express myself in this book: Thank you for another amazing writing experience. A special shout-out to Suzanne O'Neill, Tricia Boczkowski, Molly Stern, Jenni Zellner, Tammy Blake, Julie Cepler, Christopher Brand, and Elizabeth Rendfleisch.

Elise Loehnen: Thank you so much for all your help with this book—can't wait for our next adventure together!

My friends at WME: A big thank-you to Jennifer Rudolph Walsh, Andy McNicol, Stephanie Ritz, and Sharon Jackson.